Awakening to Now

Jack Dougher

Awakening To Now

Cover Art: 10 year old student from
Francis Center in Niagara Falls, NY

Printed in the United States of America

2008

Published by

DeSales Resource Center

Stella Niagara, NY 14144

716-754-4948

Library of Congress Control
Number:2008931917

ISBN: 978-0-9713199-9-8

To order: 1-800-782-2270

DEDICATION

To Josie whose presence
is precious to me
beyond measure.

AWAKENING TO NOW

is designed to be carried with you to help you maintain awareness of the presence of God in each moment, to transform the circumstances of each "present" into an effective sign that God loves you and is vitally connected to you, and to cut to the heart of all spiritual transformation, --the "NOW," the only moment available to you.

The author speaks from his personal experience, attempting to integrate contemporary insights, Biblical scholarship, and the Salesian spiritual tradition of intentionality, the Direction of Intention, and the Preparation of the Day.

Table of Contents

INTRODUCTION

I envision this book in the tradition of spiritual books often described [in Latin] as a *Vade Mecum* , --a book that "travels with you." It is literally a pocket book that you can refer to when you find yourself with some moments for reflection. As any book aiming at personal awakening it will take a lot of focusing and reinforcing. This practice of directing our intention toward Awakening to Now is very challenging and subtle. Each day we will find new evidence that we really didn't understand it as well as we thought we did, or will find the need to review or deepen certain aspects of this practicing in order to reap its benefits.

Because small growth groups of various kinds are commonly experienced as apt vehicles for spiritual progress today, I have decided to add a few discussion questions to the end of each chapter of this *vade mecum*. You may not only want to refer to the book yourself, you may want to discuss it chapter by chapter with your fellow seekers. Biblical quotations here are taken from the New Revised Standard Version.

The included questions are meant to be suggestive, or "ice-breakers" to discussion. I have designed the questions, too, to provide direction or perspective in order to encourage members of the group to expand the applications of the practice described in each chapter. I debated putting them in an Appendix at the end of the book but opted for the more convenient location at the end of each chapter. Feel free however, to exclude them altogether if they get in your way.

My nephew, Jim Wygand, an author in his own right has been of particular help to me in bringing this book to print. From the beginning he has offered many useful suggestions, performed the role of cheerleader, and followed up by editing the manuscript. Much thanks, Jim.

I feel a great debt of gratitude toward teachers and companions among the Oblates of Saint Francis de Sales, whom I was privileged to call *brothers* over a period of 35 years. Some were mentors of the core practices contained in this book, and others were inspiring witnesses to me of the fruits of having dedicated themselves to living this present moment with faith and love. I warmly acknowledge my debt to them for the inestimable gift of their example and fellowship.

Of particular and extraordinary help has been DeSales Resources and Ministries, Inc. and John Graden, O.S.F.S, who have guided the final stages of this manuscript and brought it to print.

Who could overlook, too, the privilege which has been mine to work with developing leaders in movements such as the Cursillos and Marriage Encounter. I have learned much too, through sharing this practice with parish leaders, retreatants and college students over the years. My wife, Josie, and I have read many books together and through our sharing have gained many insights regarding the practice of living in the present moment. I express my profound thanks to each and every person with whom I have walked this path.

Finally, I impart a confident and hopeful word to all who read this book and put it to work in each of their "day-tight compartments." These many, small steps will someday –like the mustard seed of the gospels—produce a great harvest of tranquility and love for yourselves and others.

PART A

FOR WHOM DID I WRITE THIS BOOK?

Chapter One
The Challenge of Presence

I want to begin our conversation by clearing the space between us. As the reader of this offering in spiritual consciousness, please know that the title is not meant to convey that I am living a life of complete awareness. The fact is that I've found it a strategic requirement to develop this discipline as a means to try to keep my equilibrium. In a culture oriented toward the achievement of things of outer value, a culture of working harder, but feeling less fulfilled and more stressed, it is easy to lose one's center. Believe me, I am very much with you in the struggles to live a human life in this time and place. The fact that you are reading this book, however, assures me that you and I both are aware of the paradoxical nature of the societies in which we are now living.

If my life ends today, yes, it will have been a complete life inasmuch as I have lived every moment of it, as best I could, making conscious choices such as God gave me to make. I have worked at being present to each moment and task of my day, that I might be fully alive and *there.* I believe that you are doing that, too. But, my hope is that this book will help you to do that better and more effectively. Not because I'm so smart, but because I have been privileged to receive some training and insight along the way into a way of *being* that has greatly helped me stay centered in an unconscious world. As you will discover, it is a simple way, deceivingly so, since its effects are so unerringly effective.

Without taking the following categorizations too woodenly, allow me to create some fictitious groups I have in mind in writing this book. (1) Perhaps there are some folk who have developed a way of life that is working for them. That is, they are growing and becoming ever more conscious of who they are. They are making free choices throughout each day that are blessings for them, their loved ones and the planet. This book is for them. (2) Some people seem to happily go through their days unaware that life has much more to offer than what their culture has valued for them. Material acquisitions are sufficient distraction for them from the deeper questions of life. A certain passivity pervades their lifestyle and they have little inclination to change or question. They are satisfied with surface relationships and content that life has been good to them, but have little thought about the actual effects of their choices on other people or the natural or political world about them. This book is for them. (3) Some may be professionally "religious," who have a kind of institutionalized sanctity that feels good, believing that the deity is pleased with them. They have no room in their consciousness for the God of surprises. They believe there is a divinely revealed plan for how all humans should live and to which, of course, they are privy. They believe, moreover, they have been given a divine mandate to bring others into line with this plan. This book is for them, though it may at first disturb them. (4) Some have a philosophy of life somewhat satisfying, but lacking in passion and connectedness. They don't feel "anchored" in transcendence. They experience a kind of existential dread that refuses to go away. This book is for them. (5) Others feel the need to discover something new that will help bring order into their lives and behavior. In the making of choices each day, they experience a lack of integration or coherence in how they should conduct their lives. There seems to be no center point around which their ordinary choices are arranged that would enable them to enact the good they desire. This book is for them.

Well, you get the idea! The simple strategy which this book offers fits all circumstances. It enhances every other strategy and injures none. Please read on and see for yourself.

Something Culturally Amiss?

The news of the day includes riots and assassinations and bombings in several parts of the world. Consumer debt in our society is in the trillions and continues to rise. Each day, we read of global climate change being at odds with the way we are living our lives.

How do we keep the balance with so much irrational behavior surrounding us, affecting us directly and indirectly? Perhaps it is this question, or ones like it, that drives you to read this book hoping to find a responsible and balanced way to keep your love alive and your life on track.

Fortunately, we are living in a place and time when many spiritual teachers are available to us through books, the internet, media, tapes, e-books, DVDs, CDs. Our religious affiliations are somewhat helpful, but are usually inadequate to save us from the incursions of a consumerist and secularized culture, and are also sometimes part of the problem because these religions focus on an almighty and punishing God rather than a compassionate, justice-loving and peace-loving Word-made-flesh who seeks disciples to help establish His Father's Reign on Earth as it is in Heaven.

There are signs that increasing numbers of people are embarked upon serious soul searching. They are getting together in groups: women's groups, men's groups, NGOs, etc.; to discuss, drum, retreat, pray, read, chant, heal, live simply, raise their consciousnesses, or save the whales, I'm sure you can add more categories from your own orbit of acquaintances.

Religious fundamentalism seems to be an attractive option for many. They sense that things are not going well and seek simple answers to complex problems, often scapegoating certain persons or groups of persons as "enemies", or even God's enemies. They are of the left and right of the political spectrum and project an apocalyptic worldview. They want to bring on Armageddon and be raptured to a better place.

Hard on the heels of such movements are the spiritual materialists, seeking to wrap spirituality into attractive self-improvement packages that promise much more than they can deliver--and at a handsome price and profit. Many are helped by these movements, others however, experience disillusionment.

The way forward for the spiritual astronauts of the inner cosmos in this time and place is fraught with difficulty. My nephew, Jim, put it this way, "How do you 'spiritualize' the secular experience?" It's a good question. The fundamentalists think they have found the answer, as we have indicated. This book will contend that the answer lays both *within* us and outside of us, and that the former is the neglected piece in our time and place. The way forward will have to begin with a converted heart leading us to a transformational project in and for this world, and not out of this world.

Ours is a response to the call to a new consciousness, including a *way* to awaken to it. *Why* this book presents a truly valuable strategy in acquiring this inner awakening, I will share with you in the next chapter.

Discussion Questions

1. Which group that this book addresses do you see yourself in? Are you in more than one? Can you offer any other group(s) that the author left out?
2. Does your religious affiliation provide you with the help you need to find spiritual fulfillment? Why/why not?
3 What about Jim's question, "How do you spiritualize the secular experience?" Can you explain what he means? Any answers?

Chapter Two
On Becoming Aware

It is said that when Gautama Buddha came out of the forest after his enlightenment, his former disciples hardly recognized him. They asked him, "What are you, a god, an angel, a prophet? What are you?" He answered them, "I am awake." This is what Buddha means, "one who has wakened up."

In order for that awakening to occur, the Buddha had to leave off extreme ascetical practices and enter the middle way between deficiencies or excesses. This allowed him to be present to the ordinary; to be in a state of acceptance and openness. In leaving off his unruly desires, he woke up to the infinite possibilities of each living moment. In the religious experiences of the western biblical tradition, this could be called, you guessed it, surrendering to God's will or abandonment to divine providence.

How are you and I to wake up? We are not going to do it in the same way as Siddhartha Gautama. We're not going to become a monk, leave our wife and child as Siddhartha did, and devote our lives full time to contemplation and teaching, or start a new religious movement. We need some kind of subtle strategy though that is adaptable to the ordinary life that most of us are actually living.

Realistically, our waking up or enlightenment is more apt to be a gradual transformation that provides continuity between the duties of our position in life and this new-found awareness. It need not, nor should it, be a turning upside down of our relationships to persons and careers to which we have commitments in justice and caring. At the same time, we are cognizant of the fact that today more people have a plurality of careers within their lifetime than those of former generations.

The nature of this new awareness or consciousness is that it is interior. It is not so much a changing of the external forms of our lives. Rather, it is a change in our way of perceiving, our way of being. If it involves a reformation, it is of the inner person, rather than the external accents of our lives.

The gradualness of this new consciousness will probably be barely perceptible to those who share our lives. It should not inconvenience them, or make them feel uncomfortable. Others need not think us weird or experience us as difficult to be around. Sometimes, entire households are disrupted and family members are disadvantaged because "mother is meditating." It should not be the exterior form of one's spirituality that is inviolable. The meditation discipline of a monk may not be able to be integrated into the life of a homemaker and mother. Perhaps one's meditation can assume a less obtrusive form. God, after all, can be found in service to the family, too. Spiritual consciousness can come from many directions in various forms.

Although we instinctively understand that such an inner transformation of perception and being will necessarily have to move out into the societal dimensions of our lives it is our hope and expectation that it will do so gradually, and at the same time, with the least intrusiveness to others. It can be more of a leavening process.

"The Reign of God is Within You."

Jesus of Nazareth is reported by Luke (17:21) to have said when asked when the Reign of God was to come, that it did not admit of observation. The Reign of God was Jesus' metaphor for that transformation of consciousness or awareness that the Buddha experienced. (Note, that it is quite possible that Jesus was aware of the religious experience of Siddhartha Gautama for the latter lived five centuries before Jesus and the teachings of the Buddha were propagated as far as the Eastern Mediterranean shores by the Third Century B.C.E.. Moreover, there are numerous legends of Jesus being in India sometime during his Hidden Life. (Cf. as an example, my novel, Gifts From the Desert. 2005, pp.97-202.)

The *Reign (Rule) of God* [often translated as the *Kingdom (Realm) of God*] denoted a way-of-life that was totally self-surrendered to the will of God, whom Jesus knew as Father (*Abba*). The "Reign of God" was Jesus' name for the mysterious generating force in his life and ministry. It enabled him to produce revolutionary teachings such as the Beatitudes (Mt. 5:3-12) and Discipleship (Mk., 8:27-10:45). It might be said that contemporary disciples of the

Buddha commonly are referring to a very similar spiritual discipline when they speak of *mindfulness.*

And how did this Reign of God come? Mark quotes Jesus in his gospel (4:26-29):

> *"This is what the Reign of God is like. A man throws seed on the land. Night and day, while he sleeps, when he is awake, the seed is sprouting and growing; how, he does not know. Of its own accord the land produces first the shoot, then the ear, then the full grain in the ear. And when the crop is ready, he loses no time: he starts to reap because the harvest has come."*

So it seems that Gautama Buddha and Jesus were talking about the same thing, although Jesus was speaking of a more personal God.

For our purposes here, however, I think we can see that both men saw life as having transcendent meaning, and that it was carried as a seed of awareness within them. Further, it grew like a tiny mustard seed (Mt.13:32) to enormous proportions, so that even the birds of the air came and dwelt in its branches.

In cultures dedicated to things of external value, such as we have currently created for ourselves, some special discipline is needed to help us connect with the still point of our lives. Many persons are striving harder and experiencing less satisfaction, contentment and sense of connectedness.

Our habitual, excessive concern over the past and the future pollutes our consciousness with resentments and anxieties, even anger guilt and fear. It isn't uncommon to find minds preoccupied with thoughts of the past, which is over and can't be changed, and the future, which is not yet here, the thoughts of which concern things that will probably never come to pass. This is a form of unconsciousness, an abiding form of unreality, which doesn't serve us well. The question becomes, "How can we learn to live in the present moment and experience our souls?"

Becoming awake is realizing that I am not that creation of my own mind, determined by its interpretations of my own personal history. Once I am awake, the present moment becomes infinitely spacious and enfolds me in an awareness of "I am." (not unrelated to the name of *Yahweh* as disclosed to Moses in Ex.3:14). This initiates new possibilities.

The being that I *am*, is the observer of the many false selves created by my ego and *because* it is observing them, it enables I *am* to dis-identify with them. The fact that I am observing them is witness to the fact that *I* am not them. *How* then do we break out of the unconsciousness that we have gotten used to and reconnect to God's Reign where true consciousness resides? This is the question we will address in the following chapters.

Discussion Questions

1. Can/should the spiritually fulfilled life "fit in" to the patterns of the culture(s) of which we are a part? Explain.
2. Can you explain what the "Reign of God" is that Jesus speaks so much about (often in parables)? Is the *Reign of God* the same as the *Kingdom* of God? Explain.
3. Is the "Reign of God," as Jesus understood it and taught it, something that is participated in by practitioners of other religious traditions, such as Buddhists? Why?/why not?

Chapter Three
A Tradition of Becoming Intentional

Each authentic spiritual tradition proffers some special way of transforming the present moment. Life is made up of present moments. The past is gone and cannot be reclaimed; the future is not yet here. How we live *this* moment is actually the key to living well.

Some of the names for this *being in the moment* are "time competency," "the ascetic of the present moment," the "sacrament of the present moment," "being there," "being in the flow," the "power of now," in short, --awareness.

In Ch. 4, I will talk more about this, but in this chapter, I want to acquaint you with a particular Christian discipline of *transvaluating* (Christians might say, "sanctifying") the present moment through focusing one's intention. It is exemplified by a tradition springing from a Seventeenth Century, bishop and Mystical Doctor (a term which means he is a sure guide in things mystical) of the Roman Catholic Church, Francis de Sales (1567-1622).

Saint Francis de Sales was the eldest child of Monsieur and Madame de Boisy in Thorens, Savoy (geographically where today's France, Italy and Switzerland meet). His early schooling was under the Capuchin Monks in Annecy and later the Jesuits at Clermont College in Paris. He completed his education at the University of Padua in Italy having obtained a Doctorate in Civil and Canon Law in 1592, the year before Galileo came there to teach mathematics. He did the law studies to satisfy his father, but at the same time he involved himself in theological studies to satisfy himself. He was ordained a priest at Annecy, Savoy in 1593 and consecrated a bishop in 1602.

This same saint authored in the first decades of the Seventeenth Century two spiritual classics, *An Introduction to the Devout Life* and the *Treatise on the Love of God*. Later he captured the core of daily prayer and awareness from these works in a small *Spiritual Directory* which he wrote for the Sisters of the Visitation of Holy Mary, which he co-founded with St. Jane de Chantal. The central article in this Directory came to be known as the Direction of Intention (or "Right Intending of Deeds"). This way of sanctifying the present moment later became one of the cornerstones of a whole school of spirituality known as Salesian, after Francis de Sales. Several congregations of religious, by the way, have fruitfully nourished themselves on this Salesian tradition: notably, The Visitation of Holy Mary, The Salesians of Don Bosco, The Oblates of St. Francis de Sales, the Oblate Sisters of St. Francis de Sales and the Missionaries of St. Francis de Sales.

Parenthetically, I have recently wondered whether Francis had been exposed to some Buddhist teachings while at the University of Padua. Buddhism was not unknown, though for political reasons, such dharma would necessarily have had to have been disguised in the world of 17th Century Europe. This might explain many of Francis' uncommon insights into Jesus' teachings on detachment that parallel the Buddha's teachings on the need to extinguish our deluded and selfish desires. Not that other Christians and others did not teach these things, but Francis' particular way of understanding seems to have a distinctly Buddhist flavor. At any rate, this would provide an interesting doctoral thesis for some student with access to university archives at Padua.

I am relating this brief history so that you may know that what I am presenting to you in Part 2 of this book has its roots in a very deep tradition. Throughout this book I will be trying to relate this deep tradition to the many contemporary insights we are gaining about the relationship between the present moment, intentionality, and prayer. (See the references in the back for contemporary popular writers.) After all, we are living in a very different time and place from Seventeenth Century France. With some careful discernment, let's try to recast the thoughts of Francis into our own very different culture and worldview.

"Well yes, but I'm not that spiritual."

I take your point. Nor, need you be to profit from this book. But I ask you, "Is there harm in focusing present insights through the lens of centuries of peoples' experiences, attempting to live the same spiritual discipline of The Present Moment? I presume that we all naturally will take what is useful to us in our present situation and leave behind that which doesn't seem to fit us. Nevertheless, as time goes on, you may find that other people's experiences may show themselves useful in persevering and achieving the goal you have in mind.

Perhaps many of you have, as have I, encountered much talk about the distinction between spirituality and religion. I would prefer in this short book to do an end run around that discussion and emphasize the fact that ultimately we are all persons with the same fundamental needs, hopes and aspirations. The insights I am sharing in this book are something very basic. They are about living the intentional life, being more aware of what and why we are doing the particular thing that we are doing, and doing it with fuller consciousness and direction. In a way, we could say these insights are kind of pre-religious or anthropological, although they get fleshed-out in different religious contexts.

I hope the fact that I have a background in the spiritual tradition of Francis de Sales (Christian/Catholic/Salesian) won't be an obstacle to any of the readers of this book. The circumstances of the Twenty-first Century call for, I think, a certain judicious inclusivity in any approach to any *spiritual* life whatsoever. (Note, "Whoever is not against us is for us." Mk. 9:40.) I can personally assure you that any attempt to proselytize is furthest from my mind. We can see all about us the effects of exclusivity and the spirit of conquest, and collectively speaking they are not pretty.

Our times call for healing and getting to know each others' spiritual traditions. It wasn't so long ago that many thought that religion was losing it's grip and that it had little or no place in the scientific and rational world to come, but we now can see that that is not the case. Religion is too important to be relegated to an afterthought. The world won't let us. Therefore, let us proceed, examining what we say here on its own merits, whatever its pedigree, and leave aside dogmatism.

Discussion Question.

> What do you think about this distinction between spirituality and religion? Is it a useful distinction? Why?/why not?

PART B

WHAT IS THIS PRACTICE?

Chapter Four
The Importance of the Present Moment

Life is made up of present moments. As I begin to introduce you to the practice of praying the present moment, in other words, as I begin writing this chapter, it is a very significant present moment. The temptation is to forge ahead with all the ideas that are in my head and pour them out onto the paper without ever being consciously aligned with the larger purpose of which I am a part and to which I am committed in love.

The present moment is the very time, the only time, when I am in the Presence of the Transcendent. As a person of Christian faith, for me that is a personal God who is Father/Word/Spirit. For others that Transcendence may be addressed by different names for example, Brahman, Vishnu, Siva, Adonai, Ahura Mazda, Allah, Wakantanka, The All, or Isvara.

I choose to adopt, in large part, the convention of speaking in the language that is most familiar to me in order to communicate the lived experience of what I am trying to share with you. I hope that this works for both you and me. I think it will.

If I were to plough ahead with my thoughts, several unintended consequences would likely occur. I would be communicating merely the thoughts of my self-conscious and self-centered mind. These thoughts would be disconnected from true consciousness and the larger purpose of our lives. These thoughts would be lacking in the love and concern that in our more aware moments we desire to learn. They would be wanting in intention and direction on my part, which would most likely have endowed them with more life-givingness. They would be lacking in that indescribable and mysterious quality which the Christian tradition calls grace.

The present moment is too precious to overlay it unconsciously with my egoic thoughts to be disseminated under the naïve assumption that "that's the way it is." Since the ego is delusional, that's *not* the "way it is." [Egoic: though not in most dictionaries yet, it is used as "dealing with states of consciousness confined to the limits of personal identity," cf. www.egoic.com] The ego is time bound. It lacks the spaciousness of the present moment which touches eternity. Every time I resume writing it behooves me to align myself with the deepest part of my being which is attuned to the present moment. There I am aware that my thoughts are not me, that the power that runs the universe is guiding me in what I am about to do and I am free to follow that guidance. I am not compelled to play tennis with my thoughts and lob a few shots over the net and onto this paper. To help me arrive at that timeless and spacious moment there is a prayer that I say to help make me aware of the presence of God and to unite my intentions with God in whatever way this action I am initiating entails.

But before I share this prayer with you, let me speak a bit more about the nature of this present moment we are talking about.

Augustine tells us it is the duration between the past and the future,--the timeless moment where the future, which is not here yet, slips over into the past, which is gone and cannot be retrieved. The present is an eternal NOW. It is where we are connected with transcendence at the level of our *being*, where possibilities are unlimited. It is the point of awareness whereby my thoughts are observed as being "not me:" I experience this deeper self as a witness to my egoic mind acting out the delusion that it is separate from all that is. What Freud call the conscious, is really unconsciousness acting out its delusion that it is separate from everything else.

True consciousness occurs when we dis-identify with the ego and accept the awareness of Presence, or the present moment with all of its concrete circumstances, as constituting unlimited connectedness. Here we experience ourselves at the level of transcendence. We are drawn beyond our time-bound egoic thoughts and are confronted with experience and boundless possibilities. We are in the zone of creativity, inspiration, imagination and insight. Here we are more nurtured than nurturing, more gifted than giving. It's as if the world has stood still and embraced us in a belonging, love and energy which our unconscious self could never, of its self, account for or be open to.

This new consciousness, if you will, is usually so deeply treasured that we long to keep it; stretch it out into permanence. The paradox is that it is permanent. The impermanence of our time-bound egoic world which we want to make the new consciousness part of is actually the one which is passing away. Without going into it at this point, let me just say, I think that this new consciousness is what has been at some level referred to in the Christian tradition as the Christ Consciousness, or the Buddha Consciousness in the Buddhist tradition.

Can we not see, now, that true love enters our life in the present moment, provided we are intentionally aware and consent to its taking up active residence? This is the God--who is Love (I Jn.4:16)--who has been seeking us, finding us, and we Him. All that is required--and it's a lot!--is that in this moment we desire Him as our All. All other desires, wants, loves, fall into their proper places when we embrace this boundless union.

What we need to talk about next is a strategy required to move incrementally, moment-by-moment, toward this love. This we will begin in the following chapters.

Discussion Questions.

1. Have you experienced the spaciousness of the present moment? Describe when, where, how. Is it replicable? Is it prayer? Why? /Why not?
2. Is Augustine's description of time helpful? Why?/why not?
3. What is Christ-consciousness? How is it related to love?

Chapter Five
The Present Moment and the Direction of Intention

"So, whether you eat or drink, or whatever you do, do everything for the glory of God." (I Cor. 10:31)

When I worked with the Marriage Encounter Movement, I was struck by couples testifying over and over again that love is "a lot of little things." Another homely, related expression which frequently emerged and impressed me as well is, "Love is a hell of a lot of work!" I think Saint Paul was expressing this same truth when he uttered this thought to the Corinthians (at the beginning of this chapter). Doesn't it resonate, too, with our experience?

To love someone is to bring a new awareness to everything we do in relation to the object of our love. It has been said that the true value of our acts is the quality of love that we put into them. And I think it is commonly accepted, apart from romantic love, that this love is primarily found in our intentions rather than our emotions or actions. If this is true, then the question becomes for us, "How can we put our intentions into the service of our loves?" This is the question we must now address in the fulfilling of our life's purpose.

Notice that Paul, by implication, does not leave out anything from the "glory of God." Can we not agree that God is glorified by our loving Him and one another? After all, He has created us out of love and for love. "God is love, and [those] who abide in love abide in God, and God abides in [them]," (I Jn. 4:16b). Saint Ireneaus used to say that "the glory of God is man fully alive." Our scriptural tradition tells us that we are made "in the image and likeness of God," which among other things means that we are free beings. What is the purpose of this freedom but to choose to be-with (love) those who know us, and care about us. When we are doing this we are most fully alive and accomplishing our life's purpose, AND glorifying God.

It is critical to remain clear on our purpose in life as expressed in the previous paragraph in order that our lives remain on course. It was Seneca who said, "Our lives often miscarry because they have no aim. When a man doesn't know which harbor he is making for, no wind is a good wind." How will we discern which wind to set our sails for if we are unclear as to our harbor? We are destined for love and the winds of love are also the way. This is an apt metaphor for the journey.

Francis de Sales developed an inspired three-stage strategy of prayer and reflection for carrying out Saint Paul's admonition. He advised us to *live in "daytight" compartments, prepare each day by prayerfully anticipating events that will occur*, and, *practice throughout the day the Direction of Intention*. Let's now talk about each of these three stages in reverse order. This third stage is the heart of this book, so the first two stages we will postpone speaking about until we have first gotten some understanding of the Direction of Intention itself.

First, the Direction of Intention: Do not be fooled by the prosaic title of this prayer. It sounds simple, and it is, but hidden within it is a far-reaching wisdom that can mysteriously transform our consciousness in subtle and profound ways. In the Christian tradition, it is best practiced by uniting our consciousness in prayer with the consciousness of Jesus as he personally lived the "Reign of God" for thirty-three years, two-millennia ago. For Christians he is the exemplar for a truly human life. Here is the prayer, some words of which I have adapted from my personal experience.

Before all the significant actions of your day, pray this prayer:

O God, grant me a blessing. (**1*)

Through love for You, (**2*)

I offer to You all the fruits of this action. (**3*)

And I promise to bear with interior peace and meekness of heart all the difficulties I may meet with herein. (**4*)

For I know that You love me, (**5*)

And are counting on me in the coming-to-be of Your Kingdom. (**6*)

You may want to write out this prayer and use it as a bookmark on this page, so you can easily refer back to this prayer, as we unpack its various elements and meanings in the following chapter and beyond.

Discussion Questions.

1. Read I Cor.10:31 again, in context. Do you think St. Paul intended this as an exhaustive list? Is it a metaphor? If so, for what?
2. Discuss the six different elements in the Direction of Intention, as given. What are your initial impressions regarding this prayer?

Chapter Six Understanding the Direction of Intention

Please note that the title of this prayer, "The Direction of Intention," refers to line (*2) "Through love for You." This introductory clause is the heart of this prayer. This is the intention we are directing ourselves to. If we are in the present moment, we are connected with love consciousness which is providing value and meaning to our actions. In saying this prayer we are already transforming an ordinary action into one of extraordinariness through love. Need I remind you, that the ultimate value of any action is the quality of love we put into it? This is the universal and organizing principle of most spiritual systems.

After this consideration, it is important to notice that in the six parts labeled with an *, there are *four* pivotal action words in this prayer; *grant*, *offer*, *promise* and *know*. Each of these verbs contributes to the heightened awareness or consciousness that that this prayer aims at. Let's now take a deeper look at each one of these.

Grant (*1): We are asking for God's help, grace or blessing. This action we are about to do is not to be a product of our egoic mind, a kind of unconsciousness trying to secure its own well-being on its own apart from the world of which it is a part. Neither is it born of a maniacal need to achieve, get our way or to "make something of ourselves." It is not an anxious need to control the flow of events. Yet, if we are not controlling events, it is important to know that "someone is driving the bus." Acknowledging God and asking for his help is both an act of faith and a form of purifying our intentions. We are giving way to God. We are aware that if this action is to be one of lasting significance and born out of love, then we need to be connected to God and receive His help. We are reaching beyond the ordinary to the super-ordinary, if-you-will. We are connecting with our source and our destiny, but more importantly the manner in which we intend to do it is, with, in and through love. This bespeaks a blessing, a grace in order to carry it off.

Asking for God's blessing is an entirely appropriate way to begin this prayer. As creatures we bear a radical dependence upon God. We are placing ourselves in utter openness before God to receive His/Her inspirations and guidance to do something new. The Spirit of God is altogether creative and therefore, why wouldn't we want to be receptive of His/Her gracious ingenuity? The Gospels are full of examples of Jesus going off by himself to seek communion and counsel from his Father in order to find strength and direction to do God's will rather than doing things on his own. To do those actions which are truly lasting rather than those arising from habit, inclination or willful desiring, is a sign of wisdom.

Offer (*3): Whatever derives from this action, we are offering all the fruits of this action to God. We are loosening our selfish hold on the activity. We are "relativizing" our sense of ownership, if you will. Through this process of offering, we are also again purifying our intentions. We are letting go of its fruits, good or bad, in advance. We are responsible for the intention and the carrying out of the action, not the outcome. Once any action is launched it takes on a life of its own and often brings about consequences different from what we intended. In this part of the prayer we surrender all consequences, good and bad, to the mystery of God's universe unfolding. Again, St. Paul reminds us in his Epistle to the Romans (8:28), "We know that all things work together for good for those who love God, who are called according to his purpose."

Offering is a form of letting go. We are part of something bigger. The universe is "acting," and we are participating in its coming-to-be, we are not devising it. Once the fruits of our actions are offered through love and with a pure heart, then we are lighter. We are detached from (or, non-attached to) the outcome. During the civil rights campaign for Black Americans, Martin Luther King counseled that the march they had scheduled for the next day *must* take place. A successful outcome was not absolutely assured because of the forces against them, but he insisted, "We *will* march." So, too, our agency is precisely what it should be. We are responsible for carrying through on our intentions, but we are detached from the immediate outcome of our actions. These belong to God's all-seeing wisdom. Like the farmer, we plant, tend and water, but God gives the increase. After all, we cannot know with specificity what God's ultimate purpose is. The Portuguese have a wonderful saying, "God writes straight with crooked lines."

This is all part of the great teachings on renunciation found in all the world religions. For example, Krishna in the eighteenth and final chapter of the Bhagavad-Gita advises Arjuna in a long discourse why he should be detached from even his repulsion at performing his warrior duties against his relatives. Jesus' admonition to his disciples in Luke 14:26-27, to renounce their attachment to even their family members in favor of following him is not easy to understand. One must be willing to let go of his/her "wish dreams" if one is to receive the greater gift of faithfulness to God. It's been aptly said that we are *not* called to be successful, but we *are* called to be faithful. Detachment and non-attachment are the doorways to renunciation. They are prerequisite awarenesses and practices to meaningfully offering the fruits of our actions to God. Each time we pray the Direction of Intention we are loosening our grip on the outcome of the action at hand. This is true liberation, freedom and peace. To say "we offer you all the fruits of this action" is easy; to actively detach ourselves from the concrete outcomes of this action is something which calls for habitualization, or needing to be intentional over a long period of time. Furthermore, this detachment should be anticipated; otherwise, we are apt to unwittingly take our offering back by being caught napping so-to-speak. This we will take up next in the 4th part of our prayer.

Promise (*4): While many spiritual traditions bear the practice of praying the present moment with intent, the Salesian form alone has this fourth element in it. We "promise to bear with interior peace and meekness of heart all the difficulties we/I may encounter herein." It is a very useful thought since none of our actions are without some unexpected obstacle or perceived diversity in the path, which could throw us off stride if not anticipated and prepared for. "To be forewarned is to be forearmed," Francis counseled those who sought his direction in the spiritual life. Our spirit may be willing, but our customary flesh and emotions are weak.

Remember Saint Peter, who in his natural enthusiasm, declared to Jesus, "I will lay down my life for you." To which Jesus answered, "Will you lay down your life for me? Very truly, I tell you, before the cock crows, you will have denied me three times." This exchange illustrates very well the difference between consciousness and unconsciousness. Jesus is very much aware of the situation. His strength is rooted in awareness that events are coming to a crisis. He has already asked for his Father's help (*1) and has offered to Him whatever may happen (*3), through love (*2); a complete surrender of himself to even the worst scenario. He has even steeled his will by promising (*4) to "drink this cup." Peter in his unconsciousness, on the other hand, is full of good purpose, but is not sufficiently prepared to carry out such a rash promise. Like the other disciples, he is busy arguing about whom among them is the greatest, and bidding for the top jobs in Jesus' new administration. Unlike Jesus, he is hardly detached from the outcome of the coming crunch in Jerusalem, from which he fully expects a *coup d'etat.* Jesus' preparation comes from a consciousness vastly more responsive to reality than is Peter's, or the rest of the disciples for that matter. Peter's heart is in the right place, and that is required, but it is also insufficient. Such a test as he is about to face needs a great deal of non-attachment to the outcome. Even Jesus had a dread of the most probable outcome.

Everyone's life has overwhelming challenges. The time to prepare ourselves not to be wanting, is to practice fidelity and non-attachment through love, *NOW* and in the next moment, and the next moment, etc.

I find that this fourth element in the Direction of Intention is a very necessary learning tool. Without it, I often fall flat on my face when unexpected difficulties confront me as I make my way through my day. It just makes sense to be forewarned when experience teaches us that any occasion can have its surprises and delusional elements. It's one thing to ask for God's help, but another to naively assume that I am no longer required to employ my wits and experience as well. This should be done briefly and simply, however, as not to become excessively or anxiously concerned about the future. Staying in the present moment is key. We needn't waste any energy being concerned about things that will probably never happen. Again, this "promising" is a form of renunciation; we intend to be steadfast in the face of temptations to discouragement or faint-heartedness.

Those schooled in the Salesian Way are quick to recognize here the wisdom of Francis de Sales in his counseling of simplicity of heart and confidence in God in all things. It is VERY important that we don't become over-anxious or fearful in this anticipation stage of the prayer. Most of what can trouble us here will never happen anyway. There is no way we can anticipate everything, nor know which things will or will not actually happen. It is best to trust God and simply make an honest, reasonable and proportionate effort leaving all outcomes in his merciful hands.

Know (*5&*6): This *knowing* that the Direction of Intention articulates at this point is actually twofold. First of all, it brings to mind the all important fact that God loves us. Yes, we have offered this action to God through [our] love, but more importantly, God has first loved us, and loves us at each stage of our carrying out our actions and promises. Unlike Peter, who forgets Jesus' love for him, and thus denies him, through this prayer we reinforce our abiding faith that our Father loves us and will not abandon us. We need this firm ground upon which to stand.

The second *knowing* (*6) that this prayer evokes deserves some explanation. It is something that I have added to the traditional Direction of Intention. I call it the cosmological reference. I felt emboldened to do this because of the kind of consciousness modern humans are capable of living today. We are aware that the universe is expanding and evolving, and has been for some fifteen billion years. The universe, as we know it, is diversifying and complexifying. Everything in it is connected to everything else, and all beings in it have some rudimentary inwardness that allows them to participate in their own coming-to-be. Humans are especially good in this latter department—call it subjectivity, if you will.

In the biblical creation story we have been deputized by God to be co-creators and shepherds of creation. Note, that on the sixth day, when God made us in his "image and likeness," the only image we have of God at that point is that he is a creator. That's all that he has been doing the previous five days. So we are to be creators too.

The empirical story of creation which science has wrought is revelational too, in that it corroborates the biblical insight that man is a co-evolving, co-creator in an evolving universe. In fact, creation itself is an ongoing process. We grew up learning to speak of creation in the past tense, but it is actually more theologically correct today to say that God is *creating* the world. We religious educators were fond of telling a story about catechism lessons. When young Johnnie was recently asked the traditional question, "Who made you?" Johnnie, instead of answering, "God made me," answered, "I ain't done yet!" He already had taken in the fact that creation ain't over and done yet. His creation was in process and not an entirely past event.

This is why I am prompted to add this second object to the prayer's "knowing," namely, that you are counting on me, with the creative power you gave me, to participate in the coming-to-be of Your Kingdom (*6). Ralph Waldo Emerson spoke appropriately in this regard, "In one soul, in your soul, there are resources for the world."

Theologians no longer define man as did Aristotelian science, as *animal rationalis* (a rational [species] animal [genus]). A contemporary, working definition that many theologians use today is: "The human being is that creature which has the capacity to participate in the coming-to-be of his/her own future, the world's future, indeed, God's future." This is why I can be confident that adding this cosmological reference to the Direction of Intention is reasonable and called for.

I am aware that not all would agree with the arguable propositions that I have just summarized above. And much more could be said about modern cosmology, scriptural theology and Christian anthropology to make my point. I will try to do this to some extent in subsequent chapters.

As complicated as this sounds, it is at the same time profound common sense. Deepak Chopra (The Book of Secrets, p.100), with great insight, points out that, "You can't be fired from the job of creating a world [which is an integral part of spirituality]. You can't resign from the job even when you refuse to show up." With that in mind, I believe it is quite expedient to add to the Direction of Intention, "For I know...that you are counting on me in the coming-to-be of your Kingdom." I feel that a contemporary person might well think that it is irresponsible to omit it.

There you have an overview and analysis of the Direction of Intention. In this next chapter we will talk about how the prayer works in practice.

Discussion Questions.

1. "The ultimate value of our acts is the quality of love that we put into them." Do you agree with this statement? Why is this (2) considered the heart of the Direction of Intention?
2. Why is the promise (4) particularly useful in this prayer? Isn't it too "negative?"
3. Why wasn't this cosmological reference (6) included historically from the very beginning of the Salesian tradition? Why add it now? SHOULD it be added now?

Chapter Seven
Practicing the Direction of Intention:
Living in the Present As *If* the Future Were Already Here

Now that we have discussed in some detail what the Direction of Intention is, you probably are wondering, "How shall I start this practice? How shall I give it a try to see if it will work for me?"

Let's begin by recalling what I said on p.18, that I would talk about the first two stages of Francis de Sales' three stage strategy, later. We have spent the last two chapters talking about the third stage, the Direction of Intention, as such. It is time now to discuss the first two stages as context for practicing the Direction of Intention.

STAGE ONE.

"*Live in Daytight Compartments.*" We will hardly be able to live consciously in each present moment, if we are unable to focus on the present day. Our first task will be to see if we are able to discipline our minds and maintain the energy necessary to attend to the tasks confronting us today. Often we are overwhelmed with the prospect of change. It's necessary to narrow down prospective tasks to manageable proportions. "So do not worry about tomorrow, for tomorrow will bring worries of its own. Today's trouble is enough for today" (Matt. 6:34). If we see our goal in terms of changing our entire consciousness and think of it in terms of time or deadlines, we will surely be overwhelmed or discouraged. All those tomorrows will take care of themselves if we concentrate on today. If we live life well today, tomorrow is already affected. Remember once again, tomorrow is not yet here; you cannot touch or grasp it. The past is gone, you cannot change it. Today is the only arena in which we contribute to an improved tomorrow.

We are an over-scheduled people. We have developed computers to try to help us keep track of our many plans. It isn't easy for us to live in daytight compartments. Multi-tasking is a proud boast of our present generation. However, an attempt to attend to many things simultaneously cannot succeed. The same part of the brain is used in each of these tasks and so the brain's capacity is divided. We will do well to live happily within our limits. Daytight compartments are a natural planning forum and can serve us well in the challenge of being present to each moment. This doesn't eliminate long range plans from our life. It's is just that they are not part of the present task and strategy we are concerned with here.

STAGE TWO.

The second part of Francis' strategy is "*Preparing Your Day.*" We are all aware of the requirement for priorities in our life. Remember Jesus' words to Martha in Luke's gospel (10:41-42), "Martha, Martha, you are worried and distracted by many things; there is need of only one thing. Mary has chosen the better part, which will not be taken away from her." Mary's priority was to sit at the feet of Jesus and to take in Jesus' words, which were truth and life. Are we, like Martha, "worried and distracted by many things?" Each day, we can be clear about our priorities and not let our attentions be diverted to matters, which while personally pressing, would be done at the expense of more important or even essential priorities. A unique and potentially life-changing opportunity such as Mary had, to hear Jesus expound on the words of eternal life and interact with him, certainly trumped any other activity she might be called upon to attend to that day. The supper could be delayed.

Our inner purpose in life is to become aware or conscious as a person. Matters of outer purpose such as tasks to be accomplished are ordinarily to be subordinated –please note, "subordinate" does not mean "either-or"-- to those of inner purpose. The latter have to do with unchanging, permanent or soul values, the former with temporal, impermanent or material values. I have spoken of this distinction in Ch. 2. The values and inner purposes of our lives do not change at all day to day; but our inner purposes should not be forgotten or short changed in the preparation of our day, because our strategy is to be *intentionally* aware of their manifestations in the unfolding circumstances of our lives. In this conscious willing to *be there* we bring love and trust to this present moment. We begin to see each present moment as a gift of God's presence, a kind of manifestation of His will, to which we respond with a loving, "yes." This is what the Christian tradition refers to as "surrendering to God's will" or "abandonment to divine providence." It is what the Taoists call, "putting your self in accord with the way things are happening." Arabic-speaking Muslims and Christians alike attempt to accomplish this same thing by sprinkling their speech with the expression "*Inshallah*" which means "*God willing*."

I think you can sense that it is no easy task to satisfy and successfully hold together the inner and outer purposes of our lives. There is a built-in tension between our commitment to our inner purpose, and to the duties –

tasks of outer purpose-- of our legitimate state in life. Martha, after all, has a reasonable gripe. Somebody has to prepare the meal! She feels that she and her sister are responsible to do it. The question arises, "What is God's will for her in *these* particular circumstances?" She and Mary answered the dilemma differently. And we find Jesus defending Mary's choice. If Jesus' visit was an anticipated event, perhaps Martha could have chosen as Mary did, and made alternative arrangements for the dinner preparation. It takes some conscious planning and prioritizing. So, the first part of Francis de Sales' strategy of preparing our day is to help us make sure we will have our priorities straight.

Francis sees this as best done as a part of our morning prayer before we start the more physical activities of our day. It could be done lying down, sitting, standing, kneeling, whatever works for us. It might be helpful for us to have a notepad and pen handy to jot down some insights that may come to us as to how to conduct ourselves under particular circumstances that we can see ourselves encountering this day.

This prayer/preparation can easily take the form of the Direction of Intention prayer that we learned in chapter five. We ask for God's blessing on our day and on our preparation of it (*1). Through love for God (*2), we offer all the fruits of this action to Him (*3).

At this point we begin to anticipate the activities that will come up today, especially the habitually troublesome ones, so that we can develop a plan for carrying them out "with interior peace and meekness of heart" (*4). This part of the Direction of Intention is especially pertinent to the Preparation of the Day. It will gather up the challenges which are part of the content of our day, so we can make the "promise" (which is part *4 of our usual Direction of

Intention). Remember, "To be forewarned is to be forearmed."

It is not hard to anticipate those troublesome parts of our day, often repetitive, where we lose our interior peace and get into our worrying, anxiety mode, or our angry, resentful mode. These are signs that we are not present in the moment, but in our egoic mind. We are not seeing things in their proper perspective. These disorienting and unwelcome emotional reactions happen every day, often at the same time, or in the same circumstances. We lose our peace because we are caught off guard or are under the spell of naïve expectations.

For instance, if you are a mother and homemaker, 3 p.m. may be a difficult moment for you. The children arrive from the school bus, bursting upon your freshly cleaned and peaceful house. Their energy is high, anticipating their rebound from the constraints of the school discipline. Your expectation of a nice quiet talk about how their school day went, almost certainly clashes with their need for physical activity. You know from past experience that you are apt to once again lose your composure and react emotionally to their exuberant destruction of your household orderliness and your personal expectations of a satisfying chat. In your preparation of the day, you can anticipate your disappointment or reaction and ask God for the inspiration of how to best counter that happening. Then, plan accordingly, resolving to handle it better today, which may include some prior "straight talk" with the children about each one caring for orderliness in the home. Ask for the grace of remembering your resolution just prior to the children arriving home from school. Say the Direction of Intention again, at 2:55 p.m. with special emphasis on your promise, not to get bent out of shape if their legitimate aspirations clash with yours.

Little by little, this situation will improve if you make it the subject of your Preparation of the Day for a week or two. You will no longer be caught off guard and will have a much more realistic and effective way of negotiating the mid-afternoon typhoon. You can then move on into the "daytight compartment" of tomorrow morning's Prayer and Preparation of the Day, to attend to this or another trouble spot in the family's life together.

So, we see that we are intentionally inviting God to be a partner with us in living our lives with love, since God has already asked us to be His partners. We are growing in awareness that we are not alone. We are consciously and intentionally cooperating with the grace of the present moment to become a more loving mother and effective parent. Critiquing each day, our awareness of ourselves in that situation the previous day, helps us learn how to respond better today rather than react to our children in those circumstances. A kind of mindfulness begins to develop in our response to the children. Remember, it is all being done out of love for everyone involved, including God and ourselves. "To be forewarned is to be forearmed." Anticipating the difficulty and promising not to react is key.

It's our common experience that when we are in tune with life and the Spirit of God, all goes much better and there is no need for such strategies, planning, etc., But life is not always so smooth and frictionless. We are nevertheless, still responsible for the quality of our loving responses to others even when we might like to react egoistically. Ultimately, we hope to live lovingly, simply and spontaneously, in all circumstances. But, in the meantime, there are ways in which we can discipline ourselves to live habitually in that moment where God dwells with gifts far superior to what we could ever do on our own. It really is a case of coming to true awareness of who we are. This is our inner purpose, to become aware.

Discussion Questions

1. What are the three stages in Francis de Sales' three part strategy for living in awareness? What is your reaction to them? Are they practical?
2. Are there emotional benefits to employing these strategies? What are they?
3. How do you think these strategies can help you become aware of presence in your life? What or who are the presences in your life?

Chapter Eight
Praying Our 'Right Intending of Deeds'

How does the practicing of this prayer work out in our day-to-day living? In this chapter I would like to give you a feel for this Direction of Intention (or Right Intending of Deeds) as we attempt to grow in consciousness of *what* we are doing, *why* we are doing it and how we are doing it. This will necessarily include the questions of *when*, *where* and *with whom*, since it is our contention that this prayer touches every aspect of our lives. It is the attempt to put love into our every behavior and thought. I will try to describe my own personal experience of success and stumbling in my checkered effort to "wake up" to the possibilities of the present moment. This is a faith endeavor because I don't think any human being will get very far taking the above goal seriously unless he/she is convinced that God is calling her/him to this endeavor and graciously enabling her/him to actively participate in this awakening and transformation: in other words, that this new consciousness is part of our heritage and fulfillment as a called creature.

This prayer begins with our preparation of the day. This day can be looked upon as a collective action, and the same six elements of the Direction of Intention can come into play in our morning prayer. I have spoken of this in the previous chapter, particularly with regard to anticipating difficult, repetitive areas of our days that require a strategy to counteract our falling back into negative, unconscious patterns.

Both Paul of Tarsus and Francis of Sales counsel us to say this Direction of Intention as many times as seems fit throughout each day. It's not so much the formal words of the prayer that are important, but rather, the turning to God and becoming aware of what we are about to do. St. Bernard of Clairvaux had the habit of saying to himself, "*Bernarde, ad quid venisti?*" ([Latin for] Bernard, for what have you come [to this moment]?) Through such advertence one is becoming more truly present to God and to this moment as a gift from God. One is able to stir up love and confidence in God, which will be very useful in doing this action well and avoiding unexpected challenges. We are never acting alone.

It is advantageous to do this not only in the large and significant actions of our day, but even in small and seemingly inconsequential moments of our day. The form of the prayer can be varied and tailored to the particular action. For instance the Direction of Intention presented in this book on pg. 23 might be employed in the more significant actions and shorter aspirations might be uttered from our hearts simply as reminders of the presence of God in this particular action. Examples of shorter prayers might be: "Yes, Lord," "Through you, with you and in you" (You meaning God, or Jesus of Nazareth, or one of the Bodhisattvas), or "Thank you, God." The effect of such praying is a strengthening of spirit, will and intention to do this present action with God's help and blessing, directing the fruits of this action toward the greater good of God's creation.

It might be helpful to review the prayer and its six actionable elements so you can capture them in spontaneous expressions or thoughts of you own upon entering each action of your day. Remember the six; asking (*1) *for a blessing, offering* (*3) *through love* (*2), *promising* (*4), *knowing* (*5), and *acknowledging* (*6) *that God is counting on us [in His plan]*. Once the formal Direction of Intention has been habitualized, --then it is easy to call up each and every one of the sentiments by a simple word or thought uttered in the heart.

An apt occasion for directing our intention is on the way to a meeting or to work. Often it is in the car, since many things today involve travel. The upcoming engagement may be one that we have prayed about in our morning prayer, because it's an area of life where negative emotions have often gotten the upper hand and we are likely to be carrying a lot of baggage to the upcoming engagement. In other words, we are employing a strategy which has both remote and proximate components. Speaking of being in the present moment while driving the car, Thich Nhat Hanh, the Vietnamese Buddhist monk has a wonderful book (Present Moment, Wonderful Moment., Berkeley,

CA: Parallax Press, 1990) in which he speaks about *gathas* written by Du Ti, a Chinese Meditation Master which are portals to the present moment. It is a delightful book, which I recommend to you because they are excellent examples of how this practice of the Present Moment can be creatively morphed into inspiring verses to transform each moment of your day.

So we see that the use of this prayer is not limited to problem areas of our life only. Any time we "rightly intend our deeds" we strengthen our presence in the here and now. We add weight to the value of the action; we add love, impulse, goodness and intent to whatever we are doing. Simply by being in the moment we experience more peace, joy and fulfillment. We find ourselves in dialog with the power that runs the universe. It isn't a burden to do this; it is as easy as breathing in an out. It's more a consciousness than another thing to do. It actually saves us from analyzing and objectifying life into a series of "things-to-be-done." We begin to understand that how we do things makes a whole lot of difference. If it makes no difference, then I suggest it's not worth doing.

If the aim of the Direction of Intention is a transformed consciousness--and it is--then we should not be surprised that it will require a challenging and long-term commitment. I have spent large chunks of my life living unconsciously, with little thought of praying my way into the moment. I have been deluded into thinking that I am doing quite well, thank you, and have thought of the task at hand as a solo endeavor entirely under my personal control. I have gained a certain satisfaction from doing things this way but lived to regret it. Such ways of behaving have neither contributed ultimately to my personal satisfaction nor to the benefit of my fellow man. Rather, they have contributed to my being trapped into a world of my own egoic projections, one which has exhausted me and brought very mixed blessings to others.

On the other hand, I have always been able to turn back to a more conscious way of acting by re-committing to the discipline of "rightly intending my deeds." It has been a liberating and fruitful experience. The point is, that one has to be determined to persevere in developing the good habit of entering each moment with the six actionable intents and attitudes that the Direction of Intention fosters (ref. again to the end of Chapter 5 or to a page-marker with the prayer written out on it). It is not magical; it is not easy; it is not a silver bullet. It is only one, albeit an effective portal into the NOW. For a theistic person it is a way of uniting one's self with God, so that one is not acting alone or apart from divine guidance.

Discouragement is always a problem in attempting anything as ambitious and far-reaching as sanctifying each present moment. One has to be prepared to forgive oneself a million times, to never waste any time on self pity or self recriminations, saying to ourselves, "There you go again, you can't do anything right!" Simplicity, humility and confidence in God are a great three-legged stool underpinning our perseverance in the Direction of Intention. One has to have no room for discouragement, which accomplishes nothing and feeds off of our ego.

Everyone has his or her own way of learning how to practice this Direction of Intention. Life itself will teach you how to draw it into the rhythm of your own life. For me, being amongst nature provides many inspirations. The animals and vegetation are examples of being in the present moment:

> "Look at the birds of the air; they neither sow nor reap nor gather into barns, and yet your Heavenly Father feeds them. Are you not of more value than they? And can any of you by worrying add a single hour to your span of life? And why do you worry about clothing? Consider the lilies of the field, how they grow; they neither toil nor spin, yet I tell you, even Solomon in all his glory was not clothed like one of these. But if God so clothes the grass of the field, which is alive today and tomorrow is thrown into the oven, will he not much more clothe you—you of little faith? Therefore, do not worry, saying, 'What will we eat?' or 'What will we drink?' or 'What will we wear?' For it is the Gentiles who strive for all these things; and indeed your heavenly Father knows that you need all these things. But strive first for the kingdom of God and his righteousness, and all these things will be given to you as well.

So do not worry about tomorrow, for tomorrow will bring worries of its own. Today's trouble is enough for today." (Mt. 6:25-34)

Modern humans sometimes have an exaggerated notion of our difference from other creatures. It is a deluded mind today that thinks we are not a part of nature, but somehow rather are a totally different substance from it.

The other-than-human can teach us a great deal about the reality of creaturely existence. In fact, I find that the act of intentional observing of nature is itself a portal to the now. To be in touch with nature is a boon to we modern humans being able to be present and to surrender to the now, especially when we do it in the context of the Direction of Intention.

Discussion Questions.

1. Does this chapter present you with an introduction to practicing this method which you feel is doable for you? Can you foresee any difficulties?
2. Would it be helpful to you to have one, two or three companions who are beginning this practice around the same time, so you could learn from one another? Would females and males be apt to have different experiences in implementing what the author has suggested? Is that good/bad or indifferent?
3. When or where do you think you might have a special need to practice this Direction of Intention?

Chapter Nine
A Metaphor for Our Action in the Present Moment

She flies through the air with the greatest of ease.

We need a picture for our mind's eye of what's happening when we attempt to act in the present moment. The one that comes to me is that of an aerial artist on a trapeze. We've been talking about the present moment as that razor-thin existing moment where the past is gone, not to be recovered; and the future is not here yet.

The trapeze artist reaches a decisive moment in her performance when she must let go of one trapeze bar and reach for the bar approaching from the opposite direction. The thrilling part is that the ropes are carefully placed and measured so that the space between the bars at that crucial moment of transference is such that the artist cannot reach the oncoming bar without first letting go of the bar she is presently holding on to. There is a moment when the one bar is relinquished --and there is no going back-- and the future bar is not yet in her grasp. There is an instant of scary decision, --to let go of one bar while not being in possession of the next! This moment of courageous decision is made over and over again during the performance, with the help of partners who keep the approaching bar timed perfectly, so it will be within reach as the artist flies through the air between bars. This moment of truth is the peak instant in her performance. She seems to be suspended in a moment of timelessness, free do something fantastical before she grasps the oncoming bar.

This is a useful metaphor, or analogy, for the existential moment in which our actions actually take place. I think this is the moment of full aliveness when we make intentional our letting go and trusting God or the unfolding universe to sustain us in *this* present moment of openness, indeed of abandonment to authentic existence. Perhaps any other sense of being in control of life, or standing on firm ground, --to mix the metaphor--, is strictly delusional. The same law of gravity is operating on the trapeze artist while she is in possession of the bar as operates while she moves between one bar and the other. The difference is that while she is in possession of the bar we think of her existence as secure, and while between bars we think of her as at risk. Yet it is the same Ground of Existence which sustains her in both situations. With regard to her *being*, nothing has changed. But that moment of "letting go" has placed her in a new moment of awareness. We might call it extra-ordinary consciousness.

Like all metaphors, this one limps. It is analogous to our acting in the present moment while directing our intention with love, it provides us with some understanding; but it falls short of conveying the metaphysical dimension essential to our present exercise. Nevertheless, I include it here as help to our understanding the importance of the present moment.

Discussion Questions

1. What are the strengths and weaknesses of this metaphor?
2. Can you think of a better metaphor or analogy for what we are trying to convey by the Direction of Intention as a prayer?

Chapter Ten
Being a Faithful Witness

Ultimately, our awakening is not a solo enterprise. It is possible that some could have the impression at this point, that the practice of the Direction of Intention and awakening to the now is concerned only with the inner dimension of our personal, spiritual development. This would be a calamitous conclusion. The human life is never a solitary endeavor, neither in its being lived nor in its purpose. To be in the present moment is to be in that infinite connectedness and spaciousness whereby we are grasped by love to live a life of benevolence. We are called by God to live a life of union with him, his creation.

I was impressed back in the early '70s by a question addressed to Daniel Berrigan by a reporter. Daniel and his brother Phillip along with others were engaging in anti-war protests which involved civil disobedience, for which they went to jail. The reporter asked, "Just what is that you and your brother are trying to do anyway?" He responded, "Oh, We're just trying to do simple things like break bread and share wine, build a community and make it available to history. That's all anyone can do." But the point he was making so eloquently was that we can all do that much, and indeed our humanity may require it of us.

Certainly, highly evolved beings throughout the planet today are waking up to the fact that our action in the world on behalf of justice, peace, love, freedom, truth, reconciliation and unity is not optional. It is possible, needed and even expected of us by our neighbors and children, and I dare say, our creator. Would our human journey be complete if we left no footprint behind when we departed this earth? Yes, there will have been "one less rascal in the world," --there's something to be said for that. But are we not capable of enacting much more than that? I would venture to say that the individuals you and I feel most connected to are those such as Mother Theresa and Martin Luther King, Jr. who have been a blessing to us all by their commitment to the aforementioned values which Jesus of Nazareth understood as the "Reign of his Father," [and for which he died]. This practice of the Direction of Intention we have been talking about is a method for helping us become self-surrendered to that over-arching project.

If discouragement is a temptation in trying to always live in the present moment with regard to our intentions and interior awareness, how much more will we be tempted to discouragement when we consider living justly in an unjust world; living peacefully in a violent world; living freely in an addictive world; truthfully in a deceitful world; unified in a fractious world? Western, social and political arrangements in modern, globalizing cultures of our time and place do little to support such life styles, and in fact, are often lacking in due ethical considerations.

Yet, to be awake to the now is NOT to be disengaged from cultural challenges. Rather, it strengthens us to be faithful witnesses and effective change agents for the good. The inner transformation that takes place in us affectively through the practice offered in this book is for the sake of benevolence, --doing some good in and for this world.

Recall the 5th and 6th part of our prayer;

For I know that you love me, (5)
And are counting on me in the
coming-to-be of your Kingdom. (6)

This *New Earth* or *New Society* is even now coming-to-be, it just needs our participation. Each time we live in the present AS IF the future were already here we, in fact, usher it in. Actually this is not a new concept. One can find its seeds in the Prophet of the Exile of the Israelites in Babylon (Is. 43:18): "Do not remember the former things, or consider the things of old. I am about to do a new thing; [even] now it springs forth, do you not perceive it?"

Discussion Questions

1. Brainstorm the number of activities in your day that can be brought under the sway of this prayer of raising your awareness and directing your intention. Can you think of any that would not qualify? If not, why not?
2. Why is detachment from the outcome of our intended actions so important?

3. Is it naive to think that "Awakening to Now" can possibly change the way the world works? Why/why not?
4. What virtue, or virtues do you think this way of life will ask of you? Do you want to go there? Why/why not?

Suggested Supplementary Readings

Chapter Four

Eckhart Tolle. The Power of Now. Novato, CA: New World Library, 1994. (Esp. Ch.3, "Moving Deeply into the Now," pp. 47-70 and Ch.5,; "The State of Presence," pp. 93-106.)

Dyer, Wayne. The Power of Intention. Carlsbad, CA: Hay House Inc., 2004. (Ch. 8, pp.147-162, "It is My Intention to: Live My Life on Purpose.")

Chapter Five

Chopra, Deepak. The Seven Laws of Spiritual Success. Novato, CA: New World Library, 1994. (Ch. 6, "The Law of Detachment," pp.83-92.)

_____. *The Book of Secrets*, N.Y.C. Three Rivers Press, 2004. (Secret #12, "There Is No Time But Now," pp. 197-212)

Chapter Six

Lawrence, Brother. The Practice of the Presence of God. http://www.gutenberg.org/etext/13871

Chopra, Deepak. Power, Freedom and Grace. San Rafael, CA: Amber-Allen Publishing, 2006. (Ch.10,

"What is freedom and how do I experience it?" pp.163-184.)

Chapter Seven

Kirvan, John. *Set Your Heart Free: The Practical Spirituality of St. Francis de Sales*. Notre Dame, Indiana 46556, 1997.

Wright, Wendy. *Heart Speaks to Heart: The Salesian Tradition*, Maryknoll, NY: Orbis Books, 2004. Especially pages 138 – 154.

Chapter Eight

Tolle, Eckhart. A New Earth. New York: Dutton, 1999. (Ch.7, "Finding Who You Truly Are.")

Chapter Ten

Ceresko, Anthony R. *Salesian Studies*, "St. Francis de Sales' 'Spiritual Directory' for a New Century: Re- Interpreting the 'Direction of Intention.'" (Originally published in the Indian Journal of Spirituality, 14/4, 2001: 377-391). http://www.desales.edu/SCFS/Studies/Ceresko

There are many Salesian resources on the spiritual family that is today called Salesian and many links. You can start at www.desalesresource.org if you'd like.

About the Author...

Jack Dougher was a lifelong student of St. Francis de Sales and practitioner of Salesian Spirituality. He had most recently been teaching in the areas of philosophy and religion at Saint Leo University and Thomas Nelson Community College in Tidewater, Virginia. In a real sense this book recapitulates his interior journey while practicing the Direction of Intention which he saw at the heart of Francis de Sales' practical daily spirituality. Jack died suddenly in September of 2012. May he rest in peace.